Orcas Ur

Mysteries of the Ocean's Apex Predators

To the Orcas,

Majestic, mysterious, and enduring, you are the guardians of the deep blue, the enchanting spirits of the ocean's depths. Your presence inspires awe, your intelligence humbles us, and your resilience fuels our determination to protect your magnificent realm. This book is dedicated to you, the ambassadors of the sea, as a testament to our commitment to safeguard your home and ensure your legacy continues to grace our planet's waters.

With admiration and respect,

Charlotte

The Majesty of Orcas: An Introduction

In the vast expanses of the world's oceans, few creatures command the same awe and respect as the orca, or the killer whale. These magnificent marine mammals are true apex predators of the seas, captivating human hearts and scientific curiosity alike. With their sleek black-and-white bodies, striking dorsal fins, and powerful presence, orcas are both enigmatic and enthralling. Orcas, scientifically known as Orcinus orca, belong to the family Delphinidae, making them close relatives of dolphins. Yet, their sheer size and distinct characteristics set them apart. These majestic beings can reach lengths of up to 30 feet and weigh as much as 22,000 pounds, making them the largest members of the dolphin family. One of the most iconic features of orcas is their striking coloration. Their bodies are predominantly black, with contrasting white patches and a crisp white underside. These distinct markings vary from individual to individual, aiding researchers in identifying and studying them in the wild. But it's not just their appearance that makes them remarkable; it's their complex social structures, intelligence, and remarkable hunting prowess that truly define them.

The orca's social structure is nothing short of awe-inspiring. They live in tightly-knit, matrilineal family groups known as pods. These pods can consist of several generations of orcas, with the eldest female, or matriarch, typically leading the group. Bonds within these pods are exceptionally strong, with members collaborating in hunting, protecting their young, and communicating through a sophisticated system of clicks, whistles, and calls. These vocalizations are unique to each pod, serving as a form of identity and communication within their close-knit community. While orcas' social structure is fascinating, their intelligence is equally captivating. They possess exceptionally large brains relative to their body size, rivaling some of the smartest creatures on Earth, including humans. Their problem-solving abilities, advanced communication, and capacity for learning have left scientists astounded. In the wild, they demonstrate remarkable hunting strategies, often working together to corral and capture prey, such as schools of fish or even seals resting on ice floes.

Orcas are true apex predators, earning their nickname, "killer whale," from their formidable hunting skills. Despite their immense size, they are agile and swift in the water, able to reach speeds of up to 34 miles per hour when pursuing prey. These apex predators are opportunistic feeders, with a diet that varies depending on their geographic location and available food sources. They are known to consume a wide range of marine life, including fish, squid, sea lions, and even other whales. Their adaptability and intelligence make them masters of the ocean's food chain. Their global distribution spans almost every ocean on the planet, from the icy waters of the Arctic to the temperate seas of the Southern Hemisphere. These diverse habitats have led to the emergence of distinct orca ecotypes, each adapted to their specific environment and prey. From the transient orcas that roam in search of marine mammals to the resident orcas with a penchant for fish, their adaptability is nothing short of astounding.

As we delve deeper into the world of orcas, this book will explore their origins, evolution, and cultural significance, unraveling the mysteries of their communication, and shedding light on the complex issues surrounding their captivity and conservation. From their enduring presence in mythology to their critical role as bioindicators of ocean health, orcas are more than just creatures of the sea; they are symbols of the majesty and fragility of our planet's interconnected ecosystems.

Origins and Evolution of Orcas

To comprehend the marvel of orcas, one must embark on a journey through time and unravel the complex tapestry of their origins and evolution. The history of these enigmatic creatures spans millions of years, shaped by the relentless forces of natural selection and the ever-changing dynamics of the marine world.

Orcas, scientifically classified as Orcinus orca, belong to the order Cetacea, a group that encompasses all whales, dolphins, and porpoises. Within this vast order, orcas are members of the family Delphinidae, making them close relatives of dolphins. But their evolution has taken a distinct path, leading them to become the apex predators of the ocean.

The earliest ancestors of modern cetaceans were land-dwelling mammals, much like today's terrestrial mammals. These prehistoric creatures ventured into the water millions of years ago, adapting to their aquatic environment over time. The transition from land to sea was a profound shift, marked by gradual changes in anatomy and behavior.

Orcas' ancestors likely belonged to a lineage of early cetaceans known as archaeocetes. These ancient cetaceans possessed features reminiscent of both land mammals and their fully aquatic descendants. Over the eons, evolution sculpted these creatures into forms better suited for life in the ocean.

The exact lineage that gave rise to orcas is still a subject of scientific investigation. However, their closest relatives within the Delphinidae family include species like the false killer whale (Pseudorca crassidens) and the pygmy killer whale (Feresa attenuata). Genetic studies and anatomical comparisons have provided valuable insights into the relationships between these species.

Orcas themselves emerged as a distinct species approximately 1 to 2 million years ago. Fossil evidence reveals the presence of orca-like creatures in the fossil record, offering glimpses into the early stages of their evolution. These ancient ancestors likely displayed a range of adaptations that eventually led to the development of the iconic killer whale we know today.

One of the key drivers of orca evolution has been their specialized diet. Orcas are opportunistic predators, capable of preying on a wide variety of marine species. This adaptability has been a critical factor in their success as a species. Over time, their hunting strategies and anatomy have evolved to suit their diverse prey, from fish to marine mammals.

Social structures also played a pivotal role in orca evolution. The development of tight-knit family pods, characterized by cooperative hunting and communication, has been a hallmark of their success as apex predators. These social bonds facilitated the transmission of knowledge and hunting techniques across generations, contributing to the refinement of their unique culture.

Throughout their evolutionary history, orcas have navigated changing oceans and shifting ecosystems. They have adapted to cold polar waters, navigated tropical seas, and ventured into the deep blue expanses of open ocean. Their adaptability, intelligence, and resilience have allowed them to thrive in diverse environments.

Orca Species and Subspecies

The world of orcas is a tapestry woven with diversity, where various species and subspecies of these magnificent creatures have evolved to thrive in distinct environments across the globe. As we delve into the intricate web of orca taxonomy, we uncover the richness of their genetic diversity and their ability to adapt to a wide range of habitats.

At the highest level of classification, all orcas belong to a single species known as Orcinus orca. However, within this species, there exists a fascinating array of ecotypes, each adapted to its unique ecological niche. These ecotypes are often referred to as "subspecies," although some experts argue that the term "ecotype" more accurately reflects the distinct behaviors, diets, and physical characteristics of these groups.

One of the most well-known orca ecotypes is the "resident" or "fish-eating" orca (Orcinus orca). These orcas are primarily found in the coastal waters of the North Pacific, particularly along the west coast of North America and in the waters of the North Atlantic. Their diet consists mainly of fish, with a particular affinity for salmon. Resident orcas are known for their striking black-and-white coloration and are famous for their close-knit family pods, which exhibit strong matrilineal bonds.

In contrast to the resident orcas, there are the "transient" or "mammal-eating" orcas. These ecotypes have a more varied diet, which includes seals, sea lions, and other marine mammals. They are found in the same regions as resident orcas but have distinct social structures and hunting strategies. Transient orcas often travel in smaller, less stable groups and do not form the same enduring matrilineal pods seen in residents.

Another ecotype of orcas is the "offshore" orcas. These elusive orcas inhabit the open ocean and are less well-studied than their coastal counterparts. Their diet consists of a wider range of prey, including fish and squid. They tend to roam in larger groups, making them a unique and somewhat mysterious subset of orca populations.

Moving across the globe, we encounter the "type D" or "subantarctic" orcas. These orcas were only recently identified as a distinct ecotype. They are characterized by their small size, bulbous foreheads, and unique saddle patch markings behind their dorsal fins. They are known to inhabit the icy waters of the Southern Ocean, where they likely prey on fish and squid.

Within the Southern Ocean, there is also the "type A" or "Antarctic" orca ecotype. These orcas are known for their striking black coloration and are believed to primarily feed on seals and other marine mammals. They exhibit a more solitary lifestyle compared to other ecotypes.

In addition to these primary ecotypes, there are further distinctions within each group. For example, the resident orcas of the North Pacific are divided into Northern and Southern resident populations, each with its own set of family pods and dialects of vocalizations. These distinctions emphasize the remarkable diversity and adaptability of orcas within their respective ecotypes.

As our understanding of orca genetics and behavior deepens, the classification and taxonomy of these creatures continue to evolve. Recent advances in genetic research have revealed previously unknown complexities within orca populations, shedding new light on their relationships and evolutionary history.

In the world of orcas, the boundaries between species and subspecies are not rigid but rather fluid, reflecting the dynamic nature of these remarkable marine mammals. Their ability to adapt to diverse environments and develop distinct cultures within their ecotypes is a testament to the adaptability and resilience of these apex predators.

Orcas in Mythology and Culture

Throughout human history, the presence of orcas in the world's oceans has stirred the imagination and left an indelible mark on the cultural and mythological tapestry of various societies. Revered and feared, admired and respected, these majestic marine mammals have woven their way into the stories, beliefs, and art of diverse cultures around the globe.

In the indigenous cultures of the Pacific Northwest, where orcas have long been a prominent part of the coastal landscape, these creatures hold a special place in mythology. For many Native American tribes, orcas are seen as powerful spirits, often associated with transformation and protection. The killer whale, with its striking black-and-white coloration, has inspired indigenous art, totem poles, and ceremonial masks, serving as a symbol of strength and community.

In the mythology of the Haida people, who inhabit the coastal regions of what is now British Columbia, Canada, the orca is often depicted as a shape-shifting creature. According to Haida legend, orcas can take on human form, and encounters with them are considered both mysterious and potentially transformative experiences.

The Maori people of New Zealand have their own unique relationship with orcas, which they call "kahu," "whai," or "tupoupou." In Maori culture, orcas are associated with guardian spirits, and they are believed to guide the spirits of the deceased on their journey to the afterlife. Orcas are also linked to the god of the sea, Tangaroa, and are revered as protectors of sailors.

In contrast to the reverence shown by some indigenous cultures, the ancient Greeks held a more complex view of these creatures. The Greeks referred to them as "orcas," meaning "belonging to the realm of the dead." This name likely stemmed from their perception of orcas as predators and scavengers. Greek mythology also included tales of sailors transformed into dolphins, and orcas may have been seen as their ominous counterparts.

In more recent history, orcas have become iconic figures in popular culture, particularly in the Western world. One of the most famous orcas, known as "Shamu," became a household name through performances at SeaWorld in the United States. Shamu and other captive orcas have been central figures in marine entertainment, symbolizing the majesty and power of these creatures.

The widespread appeal of orcas has extended to literature, film, and art. Books like "Moby-Dick" by Herman Melville and "Free Willy" by Keith Walker have brought the allure of these marine giants to readers and audiences worldwide. In the realm of film, documentaries such as "Blackfish" have shed light on the complex ethical issues surrounding captive orcas, sparking important conversations about their treatment in captivity.

Orcas have also made their mark on the world of art, inspiring painters, sculptors, and photographers. Their striking appearance and enigmatic nature have graced the canvases of artists seeking to capture their beauty and mystery.

In the 21st century, there has been a growing awareness of the need to protect and conserve orca populations. Environmental organizations, scientists, and advocates are working tirelessly to study these creatures, understand their behaviors, and safeguard their natural habitats. The cultural significance of orcas continues to evolve, as they symbolize not only the mysteries of the sea but also the urgent need to protect the fragile ecosystems they call home.

The Remarkable Anatomy of Killer Whales

The anatomy of killer whales, or orcas, is a testament to the remarkable adaptations that have allowed them to reign as apex predators in the world's oceans. These marine mammals are finely tuned for life in the aquatic realm, with a host of specialized features that make them formidable hunters and survivors in a challenging environment.

At first glance, the most striking feature of orcas is their distinctive black-and-white coloration. Their sleek bodies are predominantly black, adorned with patches of bright white on their undersides and extending to their sides. This striking coloration serves multiple functions. The dark dorsal side helps them blend into the depths when viewed from above, while the white underside makes them less visible to prey when viewed from below. This is just the beginning of the many adaptations that make orcas such remarkable creatures.

Orcas possess a robust and streamlined body that enables them to glide effortlessly through the water. Their bodies can reach lengths of up to 30 feet (9 meters), with males typically larger than females. Despite their size, they are incredibly agile, capable of swift and acrobatic movements when hunting or playing.

One of the most iconic features of orcas is their dorsal fin. In adult males, this dorsal fin can grow to be quite impressive, reaching heights of up to 6 feet (1.8 meters). In contrast, the dorsal fin of adult females and juveniles is generally shorter and more curved. The size and shape of the dorsal fin are influenced by various factors, including age, diet, genetics, and health.

Located just behind the dorsal fin is the saddle patch, a distinct grayish-white area that varies in size and pattern among individual orcas. This patch is unique to each animal and is often used by researchers for identification purposes. The saddle patch is thought to play a role in thermoregulation, as it is positioned over a region of increased blood flow.

Orcas possess a powerful tail fluke, which propels them through the water with great force. Their tails are muscular and broad, allowing for rapid acceleration and high-speed pursuits of prey. This impressive propulsion system, combined with their sleek bodies, makes orcas highly efficient swimmers.

Their pectoral fins, located on either side of their bodies, serve several functions. These fins help with steering and balance, allowing orcas to make precise maneuvers during hunting. They are also equipped with sensitive nerves, making them crucial for social interactions and tactile communication among pod members.

The most intriguing aspect of orca anatomy, perhaps, is their complex and adaptable set of teeth. Orcas have a set of interlocking teeth that vary in size and shape depending on their dietary preferences. In the case of fish-eating orcas, their teeth are long and pointed, ideal for grasping slippery prey. Transient orcas, which primarily feed on marine mammals, have shorter and more robust teeth, designed for tearing through flesh. This adaptability in dental morphology is a testament to their ability to exploit diverse food sources.

Beneath the surface, orcas have an intricate respiratory system. They are mammals and must come to the water's surface to breathe. Their blowhole, situated on the top of their head, allows them to expel stale air and inhale fresh oxygen when they surface. This rhythmic process is essential for their survival.

In addition to these external and visible features, orcas possess a highly developed internal anatomy. Their circulatory, respiratory, and nervous systems are adapted to the challenges of life in the water. Their large brains, relative to their body size, are indicative of their remarkable intelligence and complex social behaviors.

Social Structure and Communication Among Orcas

The social structure and communication among orcas, or killer whales, are among the most intricate and well-documented aspects of their behavior. These marine mammals are renowned for their complex societies, characterized by tight-knit family bonds and a sophisticated system of communication that facilitates cooperation, hunting, and social interaction.

At the core of orca social structure are family pods, which consist of multiple generations of individuals led by an experienced matriarch. These pods, sometimes referred to as matrilineal groups, are based on maternal lines, with the eldest female typically assuming a leadership role. The importance of the matriarch in pod dynamics cannot be overstated; she is the anchor of the group, guiding their movements, hunting strategies, and social interactions.

Within a pod, familial relationships are enduring and profound. Mothers maintain close bonds with their offspring, often remaining together for life. These maternal connections extend to siblings, aunts, uncles, and cousins within the pod. The resulting family structure is a tightly interwoven network of individuals that collaborate in various aspects of life.

Beyond the family pod, orca society encompasses a broader social unit known as a clan. Clans are comprised of multiple pods that share a common vocal dialect, indicating a degree of genetic relatedness. Clans often come together for social interactions, mating opportunities, and cooperative hunting, reinforcing the sense of community among orcas.

Communication within these intricate social structures relies heavily on a diverse range of vocalizations. Orcas are known for their extensive repertoire of clicks, whistles, and calls, collectively referred to as "vocal dialects." These vocalizations serve as a means of identity within the pod and clan, allowing individuals to recognize each other and maintain cohesion.

Each pod has its own distinct dialect, a vocal signature that distinguishes it from other pods. These dialects are learned and passed down through generations, with younger members acquiring the vocal patterns of their maternal family. The importance of these vocal dialects cannot be overstated; they are essential for coordinating hunting strategies, finding mates, and maintaining social bonds.

Orca vocalizations also play a vital role in echolocation, which is the use of sound to navigate and locate prey. Orcas emit rapid series of clicks that bounce off objects in their environment, allowing them to create mental maps of underwater landscapes and pinpoint the location of prey, even in complete darkness. This echolocation ability is a testament to their highly developed sensory perception. In addition to vocalizations, orcas communicate through body language and physical interactions. They engage in a wide range of behaviors, from breaching (leaping out of the water) to tail-slapping and spy-hopping (raising their heads above the surface to observe their surroundings). These actions serve various purposes, including communication, play, and hunting strategies.

Orcas' capacity for complex communication extends to their cooperation in hunting and feeding. They employ a variety of techniques depending on their prey, from herding schools of fish into tight groups to creating waves to wash seals off ice floes. These cooperative behaviors require precise coordination and communication among pod members.

The social structure and communication among orcas are not static but rather dynamic and adaptable. Pods may split, merge, or temporarily join other pods, depending on environmental conditions, food availability, and social dynamics. These fluid interactions highlight the flexibility of their social systems.

In summary, orcas' social structure and communication are extraordinary examples of complex, highly evolved behaviors in the animal kingdom. Their reliance on vocal dialects, the enduring bonds within family pods, and the cooperative nature of their hunting strategies are testaments to their intelligence and adaptability. These aspects of orca life offer profound insights into the richness of their existence in the world's oceans.

Hunting Strategies of the Apex Predators

The orca, or killer whale, stands unrivaled as an apex predator in the world's oceans, possessing a diverse and highly effective set of hunting strategies that make it one of the most formidable hunters on the planet. These strategies are a testament to their intelligence, adaptability, and complex social structures, all of which contribute to their success in capturing a wide range of prey.

One of the most iconic hunting techniques employed by orcas is "carousel feeding" or "carousel hunting." This strategy is often used when hunting schooling fish, such as herring or salmon. The pod of orcas works together to encircle the prey, creating a circular formation with their bodies. As they swim in a coordinated manner, they drive the fish towards the center of the circle, where they can then take turns lunging in to feed. This synchronized hunting method allows them to corral and capture large quantities of prey efficiently.

In contrast, when orcas target larger, solitary prey like seals, sea lions, or even other whales, they employ more stealthy approaches. "Porpoising" is one such technique, where they swim just below the surface and use the element of surprise to launch themselves onto ice floes or haul-out sites, quickly snatching their prey before it has a chance to react. This technique requires precise timing and coordination among pod members.

"Wave washing" is another clever hunting method utilized by orcas when pursuing seals resting on ice floes. The pod works together to create a series of waves, which they direct toward the floe. The force of these waves can wash seals off the ice and into the water, where they become vulnerable to attack. It's a demonstration of their ability to manipulate their environment to their advantage.

Orcas also exhibit remarkable adaptability in their hunting tactics. Some pods have been observed using "beaching" as a means of hunting. In this technique, they deliberately strand themselves temporarily on shore or in shallow water to reach prey like seals. This audacious strategy highlights their willingness to take risks for the sake of a meal.

Another extraordinary hunting strategy is "spy-hopping." Orcas will raise their heads above the water's surface to survey their surroundings, often for potential prey or to gain a better view of their target. This behavior is indicative of their keen observational skills and their ability to make calculated decisions when hunting.

Orcas are opportunistic feeders, and their diet varies significantly depending on their geographic location and the availability of prey. Their adaptability extends to their choice of prey, which can range from fish like salmon, herring, and tuna to marine mammals such as seals, sea lions, and even other cetaceans like dolphins and smaller whales.

Orcas' ability to switch between different prey species reflects their advanced hunting strategies and complex dietary preferences. It also underscores their role as top predators that help regulate the health and balance of marine ecosystems.

In conclusion, the hunting strategies of orcas are a testament to their remarkable intelligence, adaptability, and cooperative nature. These apex predators have developed a wide range of techniques to capture diverse prey, from schooling fish to large marine mammals. Their success as hunters is a reflection of their complex social structures, communication skills, and their ability to adapt to the ever-changing challenges of the oceanic world they inhabit.

The Enigmatic Orca Language

Among the many mysteries that surround the world of orcas, their intricate language stands as one of the most enigmatic and captivating. Orcas, or killer whales, have a sophisticated and dynamic system of communication that plays a central role in their social structure, cooperation, and survival in the complex marine environments they inhabit.

At the heart of the orca language are a diverse array of vocalizations, each serving specific purposes within their social groups. These vocalizations include clicks, whistles, and calls, all of which are produced by manipulating air in the orca's nasal passages. While the specific functions of each vocalization are still the subject of ongoing research, some general patterns and roles have been observed.

Clicks are the most commonly heard vocalization among orcas and serve primarily as a form of echolocation. These rapid, repetitive clicks are used to navigate their underwater surroundings and locate prey. The precision and speed at which they emit these clicks allow orcas to create a mental map of the underwater world, including the location, size, and shape of objects and prey. The use of clicks for echolocation is a testament to the orca's keen sense of hearing and their ability to adapt to the challenges of hunting in dark and murky waters.

Whistles, on the other hand, are associated with social interactions and communication among pod members. Each orca pod has its own distinct repertoire of whistles, which are believed to serve as a form of identity and affiliation within the group. Whistles are often used for maintaining contact with other members of the pod, coordinating activities, and reinforcing social bonds. These distinct whistle patterns help members recognize each other and reinforce the cohesion of the pod.

Calls represent the most complex and intriguing aspect of the orca language. These vocalizations are typically longer and more structured than clicks or whistles and are believed to convey more complex messages. Calls have been described as having specific patterns associated with activities such as feeding, breeding, and socializing. Some calls are used during hunting strategies, signaling coordination among pod members, while others are associated with maternal communication between mothers and their calves. One of the most remarkable aspects of orca calls is their capacity for cultural transmission. Just as human languages are learned and passed down through generations, orca dialects are acquired and maintained within their social groups. Young orcas learn the vocal patterns of their maternal pod, resulting in distinct dialects among different pods. This cultural transmission is a testament to the depth of orca social bonds and their capacity for complex communication. Studies have shown that orcas are capable of mimicking the vocalizations of other pods, further highlighting their ability to adapt and communicate across cultural boundaries. These exchanges suggest that orcas may have a degree of flexibility in their communication, allowing them to collaborate with individuals from other pods when necessary.

The complexity of the orca language extends beyond vocalizations alone. Their communication also includes body language and physical interactions, such as breaching, tail-slapping, and spy-hopping. These behaviors serve as additional forms of expression and coordination, reinforcing their social bonds and conveying information about their intentions and emotions.

While our understanding of the orca language continues to deepen, much remains to be discovered about the subtleties and nuances of their communication. Scientists, researchers, and observers are continually working to decipher the intricacies of their vocalizations and behavior, shedding light on the captivating world of these enigmatic marine mammals.

In essence, the orca language is a testament to the complexity of these creatures and their remarkable ability to communicate, cooperate, and thrive in the dynamic and challenging world of the oceans. It is a language that reflects the intricacies of their social structures, the depths of their intelligence, and the enduring mysteries of their existence.

Orcas' Diet: Masters of the Seafood Buffet

The orca, or killer whale, is a true master of the seafood buffet, showcasing a remarkable ability to adapt its diet to the diverse offerings of the world's oceans. Their dietary flexibility and predatory prowess have earned them the reputation of apex predators, capable of capturing an astonishing range of marine prey.

The dietary preferences of orcas can vary significantly depending on their geographic location, available food sources, and the specific ecotype to which they belong. Their adaptability to different environments has allowed them to thrive in ecosystems ranging from polar waters to tropical seas.

For many orcas, fish constitute a significant portion of their diet. Salmon, in particular, is a favored delicacy for some populations of orcas, such as those found along the coasts of North America and the North Atlantic. These orcas have developed specialized hunting techniques to target salmon during the fish's seasonal migrations, demonstrating their precise coordination and adaptability in capturing this agile prey.

In addition to salmon, orcas also target a wide variety of fish species, including herring, mackerel, and tuna. Their hunting strategies often involve corralling schools of fish into tight groups using synchronized movements, making it easier to capture them. This cooperative hunting behavior reflects their sophisticated social structures and ability to coordinate complex activities.

While fish may be a staple of their diet, orcas are not limited to piscine fare. Their menu expands to include a diverse array of marine mammals. Seals and sea lions are among their preferred prey, and orcas have developed ingenious strategies for capturing these agile and often formidable prey. Ambushing seals on ice floes or using coordinated waves to wash them into the water are just a few examples of their tactics.

Orcas' culinary repertoire also includes dolphins and smaller whale species. While the idea of orcas preying on other cetaceans may be unsettling to some, it is a testament to their position at the top of the marine food chain. Their strength, intelligence, and cooperation enable them to target and capture these larger marine mammals effectively.

In certain regions, orcas have even been observed hunting and consuming larger whales. Among the most well-known instances of this behavior is the predation on gray whales during their annual migrations. Orcas have developed a strategy of targeting gray whale calves, which are smaller and less experienced in evading predators, and this predation can be a significant factor in gray whale populations.

Orcas' opportunistic feeding habits extend to other marine creatures as well. They have been documented consuming squid, octopus, and even seabirds, showcasing their ability to diversify their diet based on seasonal availability and local prey populations.

It's important to note that the adaptability of orca diets is not uniform across all populations. Different ecotypes have specialized in particular prey types based on their geographic range and historical hunting strategies. For example, resident orcas in the Pacific Northwest have a strong preference for salmon, while transient orcas in the same region primarily target marine mammals.

In conclusion, the dietary flexibility and hunting prowess of orcas are a testament to their status as apex predators of the oceans. Their adaptability to diverse prey sources, combined with their cooperative hunting strategies and complex social structures, make them masters of the seafood buffet in the world's seas. They are not only iconic marine mammals but also critical components of the intricate marine food web.

Global Distribution of Orcas

The global distribution of orcas, or killer whales, spans virtually all the world's oceans, from the frigid waters of the Arctic and Antarctic to the temperate and tropical seas in between. These highly adaptable marine mammals exhibit a remarkable ability to thrive in a wide range of environments, making them one of the most widely distributed and cosmopolitan species in the cetacean world.

Orcas are found in both the northern and southern hemispheres, and their distribution is influenced by several factors, including water temperature, prey availability, and social dynamics. Their remarkable adaptability allows them to occupy a variety of habitats, from polar ice sheets to the open ocean and coastal regions.

In the Arctic and Antarctic regions, orcas are a common sight, particularly in the pack ice zones. Here, they are often observed hunting seals, sea lions, and other marine mammals that inhabit these polar waters. The presence of ice presents unique challenges, but orcas have evolved specialized hunting strategies, such as creating waves to wash seals off ice floes, to navigate and thrive in these extreme environments.

Moving to more temperate regions, orcas are frequently spotted along the coastlines of North America, Europe, and Asia. These coastal orcas are known for their distinct dietary preferences, with some populations specializing in salmon, while others target marine mammals like seals and sea lions. Coastal environments provide ample opportunities for hunting and foraging, and orcas often form tightly knit family pods that navigate these regions in search of prey.

In the open ocean, orcas are known to inhabit pelagic waters, where they may prey on a wide variety of fish, squid, and other marine creatures. These offshore orcas exhibit different behaviors and social structures compared to their coastal counterparts, often traveling in larger groups and displaying a more transient lifestyle.

The tropics are not exempt from orca sightings, as these marine mammals have been observed in warm waters around the world. Here, they may pursue prey such as tuna and mahi-mahi. The presence of orcas in tropical regions underscores their adaptability to a wide range of water temperatures.

Perhaps one of the most iconic orca populations resides in the waters of the Pacific Northwest, particularly off the coasts of Washington and British Columbia. These resident orcas are known for their tight-knit family pods and distinctive vocal dialects. They primarily prey on salmon during seasonal migrations, showcasing their specialized hunting strategies adapted to the region's unique ecological dynamics.

In the Southern Ocean surrounding Antarctica, orcas can be found in significant numbers. Here, they are known for their interactions with large whale species, including predation on seal pups and even targeting the calves of larger cetaceans like minke whales. The presence of orcas in this region highlights their role as apex predators in the Antarctic ecosystem.

In summary, the global distribution of orcas is a testament to their adaptability and ability to thrive in a wide range of marine environments. From the polar ice sheets to the tropical seas, orcas have established themselves as apex predators with distinct behaviors, dietary preferences, and social structures tailored to the unique challenges and opportunities presented by each region they inhabit. Their presence in diverse ecosystems underscores their status as iconic and highly adaptable marine mammals.

Orcas' Migratory Patterns and Behavior

Orcas, or killer whales, are renowned for their intriguing migratory patterns and complex behaviors as they navigate the world's oceans. These remarkable marine mammals exhibit a dynamic blend of movement and social interaction, driven by the pursuit of food, reproduction, and environmental factors that shape their lives.

One of the most fascinating aspects of orcas' migratory behavior is their ability to roam across vast distances. Orcas are known to be highly mobile, with some populations undertaking extensive migrations that span thousands of miles. These migratory patterns are influenced by various factors, including the distribution of their prey, the changing seasons, and their social dynamics.

One of the most well-documented migratory patterns is observed among the resident orcas of the Pacific Northwest. These orcas are known to follow the salmon runs, moving between coastal regions and inland waters as the salmon migrate. Their movements are synchronized with the salmon's seasonal patterns, demonstrating the orcas' remarkable ability to track and locate their preferred prey.

In contrast to the resident orcas, there are the transient orcas, which exhibit a more transient lifestyle, as the name suggests. They are often observed traveling over wide ranges in search of marine mammals like seals and sea lions. Their migratory patterns are less predictable than those of resident orcas, as they follow the movements of their prey.

The open ocean is another realm where orcas display their mobility. Pelagic orcas, which inhabit deep ocean waters, roam across vast expanses of ocean in pursuit of a wide variety of prey. They may travel great distances to find schools of fish or squid, showcasing their adaptability and capacity to cover significant ground in their quest for food.

Orcas' migratory behaviors also include seasonal movements. In some regions, they exhibit distinct seasonal patterns related to mating and calving. For example, orcas in the Southern Hemisphere migrate from their feeding grounds near Antarctica to warmer waters for breeding and giving birth. These seasonal migrations ensure the survival of their young in more favorable environments.

Social dynamics play a crucial role in orcas' migratory patterns. Family pods, often led by a matriarch, stay together during migrations, maintaining strong bonds as they travel. Larger groups of pods, known as clans, may come together for social interactions, mating opportunities, and cooperative hunting.

Communication plays a vital role in coordinating these complex migratory behaviors. Orcas rely on a sophisticated system of vocalizations, including clicks, whistles, and calls, to communicate and maintain contact with their pod members during migrations. These vocalizations help keep the pod together, even in the vast expanse of the open ocean.

In summary, orcas' migratory patterns and behavior are a testament to their adaptability, intelligence, and complex social structures. Their movements are driven by the quest for food, breeding, and environmental factors that shape their lives. Whether it's following salmon runs along the coast, tracking prey in the open ocean, or migrating to breeding grounds, orcas exhibit a dynamic blend of mobility and social interaction that continues to captivate scientists and enthusiasts alike.

Breeding and Reproduction in Orcas

Breeding and reproduction in orcas, or killer whales, are complex and fascinating aspects of their life history. These marine mammals, renowned for their intelligence and social structures, exhibit a range of behaviors and adaptations related to reproduction that contribute to their continued survival in the world's oceans.

One of the most noteworthy features of orca breeding is the presence of a hierarchical social structure within their pods. Orcas live in family pods led by a matriarch, typically the eldest female in the group. This matriarchal structure plays a significant role in the breeding dynamics of orcas. The matriarch often has the highest reproductive success and plays a central role in guiding the pod's movements, hunting strategies, and social interactions.

Female orcas typically reach sexual maturity between the ages of 6 and 10 years. Once sexually mature, they can give birth to their first calf, although the exact age at which they do so may vary among populations. Female orcas have a reproductive lifespan that can extend well into their 40s or 50s, allowing them to produce multiple offspring over their lifetime.

Mating in orcas occurs throughout the year, but there may be seasonal variations in breeding activity within specific populations. Unlike many other cetaceans, orcas do not have a distinct mating season. Instead, they engage in mating activities year-round, reflecting their adaptability to diverse environmental conditions.

Orcas employ a range of courtship behaviors during the mating process. These behaviors include displays of agility, such as breaching (leaping out of the water), as well as physical contact, including nuzzling and body rubbing between potential mates. These courtship rituals are not limited to the mating process but also serve as a means of reinforcing social bonds and communication within the pod.

After successful mating, female orcas have a gestation period that typically lasts around 15 to 18 months, although there can be some variation. This extended gestation period is one of the longest among mammals, reflecting the complex development of the calf within the mother's womb.

The timing of births within a pod may not be synchronized, and it's common for female orcas to give birth to their calves at different times throughout the year. This staggered approach to reproduction ensures that the demands on the pod's resources, including food, are distributed more evenly, reducing competition among calves.

Calves are born tail-first in the water, and they emerge into the world with the support of the pod. The mother, along with other pod members, assists in guiding the newborn to the surface for its first breath. This cooperative behavior within the pod is crucial for the survival of the calf.

Newborn orca calves are entirely dependent on their mothers for nourishment and protection during the early months of life. They rely on their mother's milk, which is rich in fat and nutrients, to fuel their rapid growth and development. Mother-calf bonds are exceptionally strong, and calves stay close to their mothers, often swimming alongside them or riding on their dorsal fins.

The social structure of the pod plays a vital role in the upbringing of orca calves. Older siblings, aunts, and other pod members actively participate in caring for and teaching the young calves essential skills, such as hunting and social behaviors. These cooperative efforts contribute to the survival and success of the new generation within the pod.

In conclusion, breeding and reproduction in orcas are complex processes intricately linked to their hierarchical social structures, cooperative behaviors, and adaptability. The extended gestation period, year-round mating, and cooperative parenting strategies are just some of the remarkable aspects of orca reproduction that reflect the intelligence and social dynamics of these remarkable marine mammals.

The Complex Family Dynamics of Killer Whales

The family dynamics of killer whales, scientifically known as Orcinus orca, are among the most intricate and captivating aspects of their social structure. These marine mammals, often referred to as orcas, are renowned for their intelligence and complex relationships within family pods. Understanding the complexities of their family dynamics offers profound insights into the lives of these remarkable creatures.

At the heart of orca family dynamics is the family pod, a tightly-knit social unit that consists of multiple generations of individuals. These pods are typically led by an experienced matriarch, the eldest female within the group. The matriarch plays a central role in guiding the pod's activities, ranging from hunting strategies to social interactions. Her leadership is pivotal to the pod's cohesion and survival.

The bonds within an orca family pod are profound and enduring. Mothers maintain exceptionally close relationships with their offspring, often remaining together for life. These maternal bonds extend beyond just mother and calf; they encompass siblings, aunts, uncles, and cousins within the pod. The result is a complex and interconnected network of relationships, characterized by mutual support and cooperation.

Within a pod, individuals engage in various social behaviors that reinforce their family bonds. These behaviors include physical contact, such as rubbing against each other, nuzzling, and even play-fighting. These interactions serve as mechanisms for maintaining social cohesion, trust, and communication among pod members.

The role of the older siblings within a pod is particularly noteworthy. Older siblings often assist in caring for and teaching the younger members, including calves. This cooperative parenting ensures the survival and success of the next generation within the pod. It's not uncommon to witness older siblings babysitting and even participating in the training of young calves, imparting essential life skills.

Communication is fundamental to orca family dynamics. Orcas are renowned for their diverse and extensive vocalizations, including clicks, whistles, and calls. These vocalizations serve as a means of identity within the pod, allowing individuals to recognize each other and maintain cohesion. Each pod has its own distinct dialect, a vocal signature that distinguishes it from other pods. These dialects are passed down through generations and reflect the pod's unique cultural identity.

Reproduction within an orca pod is a complex process tightly linked to its social structure. Female orcas typically reach sexual maturity between 6 and 10 years of age, after which they can give birth to their first calf. The matriarch often has the highest reproductive success within the pod, although other females also contribute to breeding.

Calves are born tail-first in the water, with the support of the pod. The mother, along with other pod members, assists in guiding the newborn to the surface for its first breath. These cooperative efforts ensure the survival of the calf. Calves stay close to their mothers, relying on their milk for nourishment and their pod for protection and education.

Beyond the family pod, orca society extends to broader social units known as clans. Clans consist of multiple pods that share a common vocal dialect, indicating a degree of genetic relatedness. Clans often come together for social interactions, mating opportunities, and cooperative hunting, reinforcing the sense of community among orcas.

In summary, the family dynamics of killer whales are a testament to their intelligence, adaptability, and capacity for complex social interactions. The family pod, led by a matriarch, forms the cornerstone of their social structure, characterized by enduring bonds and cooperative behaviors. Communication through vocalizations and physical interactions reinforces these relationships, contributing to the rich and intricate tapestry of orca life in the world's oceans.

Orcas in Captivity: A Controversial Legacy

The practice of keeping orcas, or killer whales, in captivity has long been a subject of debate and controversy. While these magnificent marine mammals have captured the imaginations of people around the world, their confinement in marine parks and aquariums has raised serious ethical and conservation concerns.

The history of orcas in captivity can be traced back to the mid-20th century when the public's fascination with these intelligent and charismatic creatures led to the establishment of marine parks and aquariums that sought to showcase them. The capture and display of orcas quickly became a lucrative business, with orcas as star attractions performing in shows that drew crowds from far and wide.

One of the most iconic figures in the early days of orca captivity was a female orca named "Shamu," who became the symbol of SeaWorld and inspired a series of orca shows. Shamu's popularity contributed to the proliferation of marine parks featuring orca performances, sparking a trend that lasted for decades.

Orcas in captivity have been trained to perform a range of behaviors and stunts, from leaping out of the water to splashing audiences to engaging in synchronized routines with trainers. These performances have been a source of entertainment for millions of visitors and a significant source of revenue for marine parks.

However, the practice of keeping orcas in captivity has come under scrutiny for several compelling reasons. One of the most prominent concerns is the ethical dilemma of confining such intelligent and wide-ranging animals in relatively small enclosures. Orcas are known for their complex social structures and wide-ranging behaviors in the wild, behaviors that are significantly limited in captivity.

The physical and psychological well-being of captive orcas has been a subject of concern. The stress of captivity, combined with the limitations of artificial environments, has been associated with various health issues, including dental problems, injuries from interactions with other captive orcas, and decreased lifespans compared to their wild counterparts.

Perhaps the most infamous incident that drew attention to the ethical issues surrounding orcas in captivity was the 2010 death of a trainer at SeaWorld Orlando. The trainer, Dawn Brancheau, was killed during a performance by an orca named Tilikum. This tragic event raised questions about the safety of both trainers and the orcas themselves in the context of captivity.

Conservationists have also raised concerns about the impact of capturing wild orcas for the entertainment industry. The capture of wild orcas, which often involves separating young calves from their mothers, has been criticized for its potential impact on wild populations. Many countries have implemented regulations and bans on the capture of wild orcas.

In response to growing public awareness and concerns, there has been a shift in public sentiment and legislation regarding the keeping of orcas in captivity. Some marine parks have phased out or discontinued their orca shows, and there is a trend toward creating larger, more naturalistic enclosures for captive orcas. Several countries and regions have enacted laws or regulations restricting or banning the captivity of orcas altogether.

The legacy of orcas in captivity remains a complex and contentious issue. While the practice has contributed to scientific knowledge and public awareness about these remarkable marine mammals, it has also raised significant ethical and conservation concerns. The ongoing debate over the treatment and captivity of orcas reflects the evolving attitudes and values of society toward the welfare of animals in captivity and their place in the natural world.

Killer Whales' Interactions with Other Marine Species

Killer whales, or orcas, are apex predators of the ocean, and their interactions with other marine species are a testament to their formidable hunting abilities and complex ecological roles. These interactions vary widely depending on their geographic location, diet, and social structure, offering a fascinating glimpse into the dynamics of the marine ecosystem.

One of the most well-documented and dramatic interactions involving killer whales is their predation on other marine mammals. Orcas are known to hunt a variety of species, including seals, sea lions, and dolphins. Their hunting strategies are often highly coordinated, involving teamwork and intelligence to outmaneuver and capture their prey.

For example, when hunting seals resting on ice floes, orcas may approach stealthily, creating waves to wash the seals into the water, where they become vulnerable to attack. In other instances, they employ a technique known as "carousel feeding," where they swim in a circular formation around a school of fish or a group of marine mammals, creating a vortex that forces the prey to cluster together, making it easier for orcas to pick them off.

Killer whales are particularly skilled hunters of large whale species as well. In some regions, they target young or weak individuals from species like gray whales and humpback whales. The predation of killer whales on larger whales is a striking example of their adaptability and position as top predators in the marine food chain.

Beyond direct predation, orcas have been observed engaging in various forms of interaction with other marine species. They are known to engage in play, often riding the bow waves created by boats and ships, a behavior known as "bow-riding." This playful behavior is not limited to their own pod members and has been observed with dolphins and other cetaceans.

Orcas are also known to interact with other species in less expected ways. For example, they have been seen sharing prey with other species, including humans. In some cultures, there are historical accounts of orcas assisting fishermen by herding fish into their nets. These interactions have contributed to the complex and sometimes enigmatic relationship between humans and killer whales.

In some regions, killer whales have developed specialized diets that involve consuming specific marine species. For example, some populations are known as "fish-eating" orcas and primarily feed on fish such as salmon, herring, and mackerel. These dietary preferences have led to unique foraging behaviors and adaptations within these populations.

In contrast, other killer whale populations are considered "mammal-eating" orcas, focusing their diet on marine mammals. These populations have evolved distinct hunting strategies and often exhibit different social behaviors compared to their fish-eating counterparts. The diverse diets of killer whales highlight their adaptability and ability to exploit various food sources.

While killer whales are formidable predators, they are not without their own challenges. They can be vulnerable to environmental factors, pollution, and human activities that impact their prey or habitat. Conservation efforts are underway to protect these remarkable marine mammals and the delicate balance of the marine ecosystems they inhabit.

In summary, the interactions of killer whales with other marine species are a complex and multifaceted aspect of their existence. Their role as apex predators shapes the dynamics of the marine food chain, and their adaptability to different prey sources underscores their remarkable ecological significance. These interactions serve as a reminder of the intricate web of life in the world's oceans and the need for conservation efforts to protect these magnificent creatures and their habitats.

Threats to Orcas' Natural Habitat

The natural habitat of orcas, or killer whales, is a dynamic and fragile ecosystem that faces a multitude of threats in today's world. These apex predators play a crucial role in maintaining the health and balance of marine ecosystems, but their survival is increasingly jeopardized by a range of human-induced factors and environmental challenges.

1. Pollution: One of the most pressing threats to orcas and their habitat is pollution. Contaminants such as heavy metals, pesticides, and industrial chemicals find their way into the oceans, accumulating in the prey species that orcas rely on. These pollutants can lead to a variety of health issues, including impaired immune systems, reproductive problems, and developmental abnormalities in orcas.

2. Habitat Degradation: Coastal development and habitat degradation pose significant challenges to orcas. Urbanization, port construction, and shoreline

alterations can disrupt their natural habitats and lead to increased human activity in their feeding and breeding grounds. Noise pollution from ship traffic and industrial activities can interfere with orcas' echolocation and communication, making it harder for them to hunt and socialize.

3. Overfishing: The depletion of prey species due to overfishing has a direct impact on orcas. In some regions, overfishing has led to a decline in the availability of prey like salmon, which is a staple for certain orca populations. This forces orcas to travel greater distances in search of food, making it harder for them to meet their nutritional needs.

4. Climate Change: Climate change is altering the distribution and abundance of prey species for orcas. Warming oceans affect the migratory patterns of salmon and other fish, which in turn affects the foraging behavior of orcas. Additionally, changes in sea ice dynamics can impact prey availability for orcas in polar regions.

5. Ocean Acidification: The absorption of excess carbon dioxide by the world's oceans results in ocean acidification. This phenomenon can have cascading effects on the marine food web, potentially impacting the availability of prey species for orcas. It also affects the health of species with calcium carbonate shells, which are a critical part of the marine ecosystem.

6. Entanglement: Orcas are susceptible to entanglement in fishing gear, such as nets and lines. Accidental capture in fishing gear can lead to injuries and even mortality. This issue is particularly concerning in areas where orcas share their habitat with commercial fisheries.

7. Disturbance by Boats and Vessels: Increased maritime traffic can lead to vessel strikes and disturbance for orcas. Collisions with boats can result in injuries or fatalities, while the disturbance caused by boats can disrupt their natural behaviors, such as hunting and resting.

8. Reduced Prey Availability: The depletion of prey species due to various factors, including overfishing and environmental changes, can lead to reduced prey availability for orcas. This can result in malnutrition, reduced reproductive success, and overall population declines.

9. Chemical Contaminants: In addition to pollution, orcas are exposed to chemical contaminants, including persistent organic pollutants (POPs) like PCBs and DDT. These chemicals can accumulate in orcas' blubber and are passed from mother to calf during lactation, potentially affecting calf survival and development.

10. Oil Spills: Oil spills, whether from transportation accidents or offshore drilling, pose a significant threat to orcas and their habitat. Oil spills can have devastating effects on marine ecosystems, including contamination of prey species and direct harm to orcas through ingestion or contact with oil.

These threats collectively pose a grave challenge to the well-being and survival of orcas and the health of their natural habitat. Conservation efforts are crucial to mitigate these threats, protect their ecosystems, and ensure the continued presence of these magnificent marine mammals in our oceans.

Pollution and Its Impact on Orcas

Pollution, both chemical and plastic, has emerged as a significant and pervasive threat to orcas, also known as killer whales, and their fragile marine ecosystems. These apex predators, residing at the top of the marine food chain, are highly vulnerable to the accumulative effects of various pollutants. Pollution disrupts their natural behaviors, impairs their health, and poses long-term risks to their populations.

1. **Chemical Contaminants**: Chemical pollutants, including heavy metals, industrial chemicals, and pesticides, find their way into the oceans through runoff, atmospheric deposition, and industrial discharges. These contaminants can be absorbed by the prey species that orcas depend on, and as orcas

consume these contaminated prey, the pollutants accumulate in their bodies. Chemical contamination can lead to a range of health issues in orcas, including immune system suppression, hormonal disruptions, and impaired reproductive success.

2. **Persistent Organic Pollutants (POPs)**: Persistent organic pollutants, such as polychlorinated biphenyls (PCBs), dichlorodiphenyltrichloroethane (DDT), and brominated flame retardants, are particularly concerning. These chemicals are highly stable and accumulate in orcas' blubber over time. When female orcas nurse their calves, they transfer these contaminants to their young, potentially compromising the calf's health and development.

3. **Bioaccumulation**: Orcas are at the top of the marine food chain, which means they consume prey that have already ingested pollutants from lower trophic levels. This process, known as bioaccumulation, results in higher concentrations of pollutants in orcas compared to their prey. As a result, orcas are considered "sentinels" of ocean health, as their pollutant levels provide insights into the overall state of the marine environment.

4. **Health Impacts**: The accumulation of chemical contaminants in orcas' bodies can lead to a myriad of health problems. Weakened immune systems make them more susceptible to diseases, while hormonal disruptions can affect reproductive success. The high levels of contaminants in their blubber can lead to skin lesions and weakened body condition, reducing their overall fitness.

5. **Reproductive Issues**: Chemical pollutants, particularly POPs, can interfere with orcas' reproductive capabilities. Females with high levels of these contaminants may experience difficulty

conceiving, higher rates of stillbirths, and lower calf survival. This can contribute to declining populations in some regions.

6. **Plastic Pollution**: In addition to chemical contamination, orcas are confronted with the growing problem of plastic pollution. Discarded plastics enter the oceans, break down into microplastics, and are ingested by marine life. Orcas can inadvertently consume plastics when they feed on fish that have ingested these particles. The ingestion of plastics can lead to gastrointestinal problems, blockages, and malnutrition.

7. **Noise Pollution**: While not directly related to chemical pollution, noise pollution from human activities like shipping and construction can disrupt orcas' echolocation and communication. Their ability to locate prey, navigate, and maintain social bonds can be impaired by excessive underwater noise, further compromising their foraging success and survival.

8. **Conservation Efforts**: Efforts to mitigate the impact of pollution on orcas include regulations to reduce chemical discharges into the oceans, bans on certain pollutants like PCBs, and initiatives to reduce plastic waste and marine litter. Monitoring programs are in place to track pollutant levels in orca populations and inform conservation strategies.

In conclusion, pollution, whether in the form of chemical contaminants or plastic waste, poses a substantial threat to orcas and the marine ecosystems they inhabit. The persistence and bioaccumulation of pollutants in orcas emphasize the urgent need for global efforts to reduce pollution and protect the health of our oceans, ensuring a safer future for these magnificent marine mammals.

The Conservation Efforts to Protect Orcas

The conservation of orcas, or killer whales, has become a global imperative in recent years. As apex predators of the oceans, these magnificent marine mammals play a crucial role in maintaining the health and balance of marine ecosystems. To safeguard their populations and habitats, an array of conservation efforts and initiatives have been established worldwide, reflecting the shared commitment to protecting these iconic creatures and the delicate ecosystems they inhabit.

1. **Marine Protected Areas (MPAs)**: The establishment of Marine Protected Areas, or MPAs, is one of the fundamental strategies in orca conservation. These designated areas aim to minimize human disturbances, regulate commercial

activities, and protect critical habitats. MPAs contribute to the preservation of orcas' natural foraging and breeding grounds.

2. **Reduced Pollution**: Regulations and bans on pollutants like PCBs (polychlorinated biphenyls) have been implemented to reduce chemical contamination in orcas' environments. Monitoring programs track pollutant levels in orca populations and inform conservation strategies. Efforts to reduce plastic waste and marine litter are also ongoing.

3. **Prey Management**: To ensure orcas have access to an adequate food supply, fisheries management is crucial. Sustainable fishing practices and regulations help protect the prey species that orcas rely on, such as salmon. Ensuring healthy fish populations is vital for orcas' survival.

4. **Noise Mitigation**: Addressing noise pollution from shipping, construction, and industrial activities is essential. Regulations and guidelines aim to minimize underwater noise in orcas' habitats, preserving their echolocation and communication abilities.

5. **Vessel Regulations**: Restrictions on vessel approaches and speed limits in orca habitats help minimize disturbances and the risk of vessel strikes. Guidelines and educational campaigns promote responsible whale-watching practices to protect orcas and their habitats.

6. **Collaborative Research**: Scientists and researchers collaborate on studies to better understand orca populations, behavior, and health. This research informs conservation decisions and management strategies.

7. **Population Monitoring**: Ongoing monitoring of orca populations provides insights into their status and trends. Photo identification and genetic studies help track individual orcas, assess population health, and inform conservation actions.

8. **International Agreements**: International agreements and conventions, such as the Convention on the Conservation of Migratory Species of Wild Animals (CMS) and the Convention on International Trade in Endangered Species of Wild Fauna and Flora (CITES), work to protect orcas and their habitats across borders.

9. **Education and Outreach**: Public awareness and education campaigns are critical components of orca conservation. They raise awareness about the importance of protecting these animals and their ecosystems, fostering a sense of stewardship among communities.

10. **Legislation**: Legislative measures at the national and regional levels are implemented to protect orcas and their habitats. These include laws against harmful fishing practices, habitat destruction, and pollution.

11. **Rescue and Rehabilitation**: Efforts to rescue and rehabilitate stranded or injured orcas are part of conservation initiatives. Organizations work to provide medical care and support to these individuals, with the aim of returning them to the wild whenever possible.

12. **Conservation Partnerships**: Collaboration among governmental agencies, non-profit organizations, researchers, and local communities is essential for effective orca conservation. These partnerships bring together expertise and resources to address complex challenges.

13. **Climate Change Mitigation**: Addressing the impacts of climate change, including ocean warming and acidification, is integral to orca conservation. Global efforts to reduce greenhouse gas emissions and protect the marine environment are vital for their survival.

In conclusion, the conservation efforts to protect orcas are multifaceted and collaborative, reflecting the global commitment to preserving these magnificent marine mammals and their ecosystems. These initiatives seek to mitigate threats, reduce human disturbances, and promote responsible stewardship of our oceans, ensuring a future where orcas continue to thrive in their natural habitats.

Orcas in the Media: From "Shamu" to "Free Willy"

Orcas, or killer whales, have long captivated the public's imagination and featured prominently in the world of media and entertainment. From iconic performances at marine parks to heartwarming tales on the silver screen, the portrayal of these majestic marine mammals has evolved over the years, reflecting changing perspectives on their conservation, welfare, and our relationship with them.

The story of orcas in the media begins with the emergence of marine parks and aquariums in the mid-20th century. One of the most famous orcas to make a splash in the entertainment industry was "Shamu." Shamu was not a single orca but a stage name used by multiple killer whales performing at SeaWorld parks. Shamu became a household name, representing the allure of orca shows in the 1960s and 1970s. These performances featured acrobatics, splashing, and close encounters with trainers, drawing crowds of enthralled spectators.

As orca shows gained popularity, the public's fascination with these intelligent and powerful creatures grew. However, it was not until the late 20th century that the portrayal of orcas in the media took a significant turn. One of the pivotal moments in this shift was the release of the film "Orca" in 1977, a thriller that depicted a vengeful killer whale seeking retribution. This cinematic portrayal highlighted the darker side of the human-orca relationship and raised questions about the ethics of capturing and displaying orcas for entertainment.

The 1990s marked another turning point with the release of "Free Willy" in 1993. The film's heartwarming story of a young boy's bond with a captive orca named Willy struck a chord with audiences worldwide. It not only emphasized the intelligence and emotional complexity of orcas but also sparked a renewed public interest in their welfare. The success of "Free Willy" catalyzed efforts to improve the conditions of captive orcas and raised awareness about their conservation.

In 1996, "Free Willy 2: The Adventure Home" continued the story of Willy's journey to freedom, reinforcing the theme of orca liberation. The real-life counterpart to this fictional tale was Keiko, the orca who portrayed Willy in the film. Keiko's story captured global attention as he was relocated from a Mexican amusement park to a rehabilitation facility in Oregon, with the ultimate goal of returning him to the wild. While Keiko's journey was challenging and complex, it highlighted the potential for rehabilitating captive orcas and sparked discussions about their release.

The 21st century saw a further shift in public perception and media portrayals of orcas. Documentaries like "Blackfish," released in 2013, exposed the darker side of orca captivity. The film, which focused on the life of Tilikum, an orca involved in the tragic death of a trainer at SeaWorld Orlando, raised ethical questions about keeping these intelligent and wide-ranging animals in captivity. It led to public outrage and a decline in attendance at marine parks featuring orca shows.

In response to the changing tide of public opinion, some marine parks phased out their orca shows, with SeaWorld announcing an end to its breeding program and theatrical performances in 2016. Legislation and regulations also began to reflect these evolving perspectives, with some countries and regions implementing bans on orca captivity.

Orcas continue to be a subject of fascination and concern in the media, reflecting the ongoing debate about their welfare, conservation, and the complex relationship between humans and these apex predators. As our understanding of orcas deepens and our commitment to their protection grows, the portrayal of these magnificent marine mammals in the media continues to evolve, ultimately influencing the way we interact with and protect them in the wild and in captivity.

Unraveling the Mysteries of Orca Intelligence

The intelligence of orcas, also known as killer whales, stands as one of the most captivating and enigmatic aspects of these marine mammals. Their remarkable cognitive abilities and complex social behaviors have intrigued scientists, researchers, and the general public for decades. In our quest to understand the depth of orca intelligence, we uncover a tapestry of fascinating insights into their world.

Orcas belong to the family Delphinidae, a group of cetaceans that includes dolphins and porpoises. Within this family, they are the largest and perhaps the most intellectually advanced members. Their brain size, relative to body size, is among the largest in the animal kingdom, paralleling the size of the brains of some great apes. This cerebral capacity hints at the potential for highly developed cognitive functions. One of the most compelling facets of orca intelligence is their ability to communicate. Orcas possess an intricate system of vocalizations, often referred to as a "language." Each pod, or social group, has its unique dialect, with distinct calls and sounds that are learned and passed down through generations. This vocal complexity suggests a level of cultural transmission within orca communities, where knowledge and behaviors are shared and taught, akin to human culture.

Communication among orcas extends beyond mere vocalizations. They use body language and behaviors to convey messages and coordinate group activities. For instance, breaching, spy-hopping, and tail-slapping are all forms of non-vocal communication that serve various purposes, from hunting to social bonding.

One of the most astonishing displays of orca intelligence is their hunting strategies. Different orca populations have developed specialized hunting techniques that require advanced problem-solving abilities and teamwork. Some orcas employ "carousel feeding," where they swim in a circular formation to corral prey, while others demonstrate "wave washing" to knock seals off ice floes. These strategies reflect a level of adaptability and innovation in their pursuit of food.

Social complexity is another hallmark of orca intelligence. They live in matrilineal societies, with strong bonds between mothers and their offspring. These social groups, or pods, can comprise several generations and engage in cooperative behaviors, such as hunting and childcare. The matriarch, typically the oldest female, plays a central role in pod dynamics, guiding the group's movements and decision-making. Beyond pod interactions, orcas are known for forming alliances with other pods. These associations highlight their ability to establish relationships, collaborate on hunting, and navigate a complex social landscape. Such cooperative arrangements underscore the depth of their social intelligence.

Orcas' problem-solving skills extend to their interactions with humans. In captivity, they have been trained to perform intricate tasks and behaviors, showcasing their capacity to learn and adapt to novel environments. However, the ethics of keeping these highly intelligent creatures in captivity has been a subject of debate and concern, as it limits their natural behaviors and can lead to stress-related health issues.

Studies conducted on wild orcas have revealed their impressive memory and learning abilities. They can remember hunting techniques and vocalizations for years, if not decades, underscoring their long-term memory and capacity for cultural transmission.

As we continue to unravel the mysteries of orca intelligence, we gain a deeper appreciation for these magnificent creatures' cognitive prowess. Their complex communication, problem-solving skills, and social dynamics challenge our understanding of animal intelligence and illuminate the intricate world of orcas beneath the waves. The ongoing research into their mental faculties reminds us of the need for responsible conservation efforts to protect and preserve the habitats of these extraordinary beings, ensuring that the legacy of their intelligence endures in the oceans they call home.

The Ethical Debate Surrounding Orca Research

The study and research of orcas, or killer whales, have been a source of fascination, discovery, and controversy for decades. While scientific investigation into these magnificent marine mammals has led to valuable insights into their biology, behavior, and ecology, it has also sparked a complex ethical debate regarding the impact of such research on orcas and the moral responsibilities of scientists and institutions involved.

At the heart of the ethical debate surrounding orca research lies the question of whether the benefits of research outweigh the potential harm to the animals. Orcas are highly intelligent, sentient beings with complex social structures and intricate communication systems. Their captivity in marine parks, where much of the early research took place, has been the focal point of this debate.

Critics argue that the capture and confinement of orcas for research and public display represent a significant ethical concern. The process of capturing orcas from the wild, separating them from their family groups, and transporting them to captivity has been characterized as cruel and traumatic. It has led to the suffering and mortality of many individuals, raising questions about the ethics of such practices in the pursuit of scientific knowledge.

Furthermore, the living conditions of captive orcas have been a subject of ethical scrutiny. The relatively small tanks in marine parks often fail to provide these highly mobile and wide-ranging animals with the physical and mental stimulation they require. Critics argue that captivity imposes severe stress and psychological distress on orcas, raising moral concerns about the ethics of conducting research in such environments.

As the public's awareness of the ethical implications of orca captivity grew, there was a shift in societal attitudes and regulations. Organizations like SeaWorld, once a prominent player in the orca entertainment industry, faced public backlash and legal restrictions. In response, SeaWorld announced the end of its orca breeding program and theatrical performances in 2016, marking a significant moment in the ongoing ethical discourse surrounding orca research.

While there is consensus that research can contribute to the conservation and understanding of orcas, the ethical debate has prompted a reevaluation of research methods and priorities. In the wild, non-invasive research techniques, such as photo identification, acoustic monitoring, and satellite tagging, have become standard practices. These methods allow scientists to gather valuable data without disturbing or harming the animals.

The ethical debate extends beyond the realm of captivity to include considerations of how research findings are used. Some argue that the knowledge gained through research should primarily serve conservation efforts and the welfare of orcas. Conversely, concerns arise when research findings are used to justify practices that may be detrimental to wild orca populations, such as fisheries management decisions that impact their prey species.

Additionally, the issue of who conducts orca research and how it is funded can have ethical implications. Research conducted by institutions with vested interests in the captivity or exploitation of orcas may be perceived as biased. Funding sources that prioritize commercial interests over ethical considerations can influence the direction and outcomes of research.

Ethical debates surrounding orca research underscore the broader ethical challenges facing the scientific community when studying highly intelligent and sentient animals. Balancing the pursuit of knowledge with the well-being and rights of the subjects under study remains an ongoing challenge. The evolving ethical framework emphasizes the importance of conducting research that respects the intrinsic value of orcas and contributes to their conservation, while also highlighting the ethical responsibilities of researchers and institutions involved in such endeavors.

The Future of Orcas: Challenges and Hope

The future of orcas, also known as killer whales, stands at a crossroads marked by a complex interplay of challenges and opportunities. As we navigate the 21st century, our understanding of these remarkable marine mammals has deepened, revealing both the fragility of their existence and the potential for positive change. The path forward is illuminated by a mix of scientific research, conservation efforts, and evolving ethical considerations.

One of the most pressing challenges facing orcas is the loss of their natural habitat. Coastal development, pollution, and habitat degradation continue to encroach upon the pristine waters where these apex predators once thrived. Human activities, such as shipping and industrial operations, introduce noise pollution that disrupts orcas' communication and hunting abilities. Rising sea temperatures and ocean acidification due to climate change further threaten their prey species and, by extension, the orcas that depend on them.

Overfishing compounds these challenges, depleting the stocks of prey species like salmon that orcas rely on. Competition with commercial fisheries for dwindling resources places additional stress on orcas' ability to meet their nutritional needs. This food scarcity has cascading effects, leading to malnutrition, compromised reproductive success, and population declines in certain orca groups.

Pollution remains a persistent threat, with chemical contaminants and plastic waste accumulating in orcas' environments. These pollutants not only disrupt their health but also seep into the prey they consume, perpetuating the cycle of contamination. The long-term effects of chemical exposure, particularly persistent organic pollutants (POPs), continue to raise concerns about the viability of orca populations.

The ethical debate surrounding orcas also shapes their future. Public sentiment has shifted away from captivity, with marine parks phasing out orca shows and breeding programs in response to public pressure and legal restrictions. The ethical considerations surrounding orca research emphasize the importance of non-invasive and welfare-conscious research methods.

Yet, amid these challenges, there is hope. Conservation efforts have gained momentum, with the establishment of Marine Protected Areas (MPAs) and the implementation of regulations to reduce pollution and noise pollution. Sustainable fishing practices and fisheries management initiatives are striving to restore prey populations. Research on orcas' complex social structures and behaviors has provided insights into their needs and vulnerabilities, informing conservation strategies.

Translocation and rescue efforts for stranded or injured orcas aim to rehabilitate and reintroduce individuals to the wild. These initiatives underscore the commitment to the welfare and preservation of these extraordinary creatures.

The evolution of public awareness and ethical considerations has inspired a collective sense of responsibility to protect orcas and their habitats. International agreements, such as the Convention on the Conservation of Migratory Species of Wild Animals (CMS) and the Convention on International Trade in Endangered Species of Wild Fauna and Flora (CITES), reflect the global commitment to orca conservation.

The future of orcas depends on our ability to address these challenges with urgency and resolve. It requires a holistic approach that balances the needs of both orcas and the ecosystems they inhabit. Scientific research, ethical considerations, and collaborative efforts must guide our actions. By harnessing our understanding, compassion, and determination, we can aspire to a future where orcas continue to grace the oceans, embodying the resilience and wonder of the natural world.

Orcas as Bioindicators of Ocean Health

The majestic orca, or killer whale, has earned its place not only as a symbol of the ocean's wild beauty but also as a vital bioindicator of the health of our planet's marine ecosystems. These apex predators, with their intricate biology, wide-ranging habits, and unique position in the food chain, offer profound insights into the state of our oceans.

One of the primary roles of orcas as bioindicators is their sensitivity to environmental changes, particularly the accumulation of pollutants. As apex predators, they occupy the top tier of the marine food chain, which means they feed on prey species that have already ingested pollutants from lower trophic levels. This process, known as biomagnification, results in higher concentrations of contaminants in orcas compared to their prey. The presence and levels of pollutants in their bodies serve as a reflection of the broader contamination of marine ecosystems.

One group of pollutants that has garnered significant attention in orca research is persistent organic pollutants (POPs). These include substances like polychlorinated biphenyls (PCBs), dichlorodiphenyltrichloroethane (DDT), and brominated flame retardants. Orcas accumulate these chemicals in their blubber, and the detection of high levels serves as a warning sign of contamination in their habitats. The presence of POPs in orca populations has raised concerns about the broader implications for human and ecosystem health.

Heavy metals, another class of pollutants, are also monitored through orca bioindicators. Contaminants like mercury, cadmium, and lead find their way into marine environments through industrial processes and pollution runoff. Orcas accumulate these metals, and their analysis provides valuable data about the overall health of marine ecosystems, as well as the potential risks to species lower in the food chain, including humans who consume seafood.

Beyond chemical contaminants, orcas are sensitive to changes in their prey availability, which can be influenced by factors like overfishing and habitat degradation. As skilled hunters, their foraging success relies on abundant prey populations. When prey species decline due to overfishing or changes in their environment, orcas face nutritional stress, lower reproductive success, and an increased risk of malnutrition.

Orcas' social structures and communication methods also serve as bioindicators. These highly intelligent animals live in complex matrilineal societies with strong family bonds. Any disruptions in their social dynamics can indicate underlying ecological challenges. Behavioral changes, such as reduced reproductive success or increased aggression, can reflect environmental stressors affecting their prey, habitat, or overall ecosystem health.

As scientists study orcas and collect data on their health, pollutant levels, behavior, and reproductive success, they gain a deeper understanding of the interconnectedness of marine ecosystems. This understanding extends to the broader implications for human health, as the contaminants that accumulate in orcas can ultimately find their way into the seafood we consume.

Efforts to protect orcas and their habitats align with broader goals of marine conservation and environmental stewardship. By safeguarding the health of these magnificent marine mammals, we are, in turn, working to preserve the health of the oceans and the many species that depend on them, including humans. As bioindicators of ocean health, orcas remind us of the vital importance of protecting and restoring the natural balance of our seas, securing a sustainable future for all.

How You Can Support Orca Conservation

Orca conservation is a global effort that requires the collective action and support of individuals, communities, organizations, and governments. Whether you live near the coast or far inland, there are numerous ways you can contribute to the preservation of these magnificent marine mammals and their ocean habitats.

1. **Educate Yourself**: Start by learning about orcas, their biology, behavior, and the challenges they face. A well-informed advocate can be a powerful force for change.
2. **Support Conservation Organizations**: Many nonprofit organizations are dedicated to orca conservation. Consider donating to these

organizations, as your financial support can fund research, habitat protection, and advocacy efforts.

3. **Advocate for Policy Change**: Stay informed about policies that affect orca conservation, such as marine protected areas, pollution regulations, and fisheries management. Advocate for stronger environmental policies and hold policymakers accountable.

4. **Responsible Seafood Choices**: Make sustainable seafood choices to reduce the demand for overfished species and support ecosystem health. Look for certifications like MSC (Marine Stewardship Council) or consult sustainable seafood guides.

5. **Reduce Plastic Use**: Plastics are a significant threat to marine life, including orcas. Reduce your plastic consumption, recycle properly, and participate in beach clean-ups to prevent plastic pollution.

6. **Support Sustainable Fisheries**: Buy seafood from fisheries that employ sustainable practices and bycatch reduction measures. Supporting responsible fishing helps protect orcas' prey.

7. **Report Marine Wildlife Sightings**: If you encounter orcas or other marine wildlife, report your sightings to local authorities or organizations that monitor and protect these animals. Your observations can contribute to research and conservation efforts.

8. **Responsible Whale-Watching**: If you go whale-watching, choose operators that adhere to responsible and ethical guidelines for wildlife encounters. Maintain a respectful distance and minimize disturbances to the animals.

9. **Support Captive Orcas' Retirement**: Some organizations work to retire captive orcas to seaside

sanctuaries. Support these initiatives to improve the welfare of orcas in captivity.

10. **Reduce Carbon Footprint**: Climate change poses a threat to orcas and their habitats. Reduce your carbon footprint by conserving energy, using public transportation, and supporting renewable energy sources.

11. **Participate in Conservation Events**: Join or participate in local or international events and campaigns dedicated to orca conservation. These events raise awareness and funds for critical conservation initiatives.

12. **Educate Others**: Share your knowledge and passion for orcas with friends, family, and your community. Encourage others to take action and make informed choices for the environment.

13. **Support Sustainable Tourism**: When traveling to orca habitats, choose eco-friendly tourism operators that prioritize the well-being of marine wildlife and ecosystems.

14. **Volunteer**: Consider volunteering with local conservation organizations or participating in citizen science programs focused on marine wildlife monitoring and protection.

15. **Engage on Social Media**: Use social media platforms to raise awareness about orcas and conservation issues. Share informative content and engage in discussions to reach a broader audience.

16. **Reduce Noise Pollution**: Advocate for noise reduction measures in areas frequented by orcas. Reducing underwater noise from shipping and industrial activities helps protect their communication and hunting abilities.

17. **Be a Responsible Boater**: If you own a boat, follow guidelines for responsible boating near orca

habitats. Be aware of speed limits and maintain a safe distance from these marine mammals.

18. **Support Research**: Research is crucial for understanding and protecting orcas. Consider supporting scientific research initiatives focused on orcas and their ecosystems.

Every individual action counts in the collective effort to safeguard orcas and the oceans they inhabit. By becoming an advocate for orca conservation and making informed choices, you can contribute to a brighter future for these incredible marine mammals and the health of our planet's seas.

Epilog

In the vast expanse of our world's oceans, where sunlight plays upon the surface and depths hold untold mysteries, the orca, or killer whale, stands as an enduring symbol of nature's power and beauty. This remarkable marine mammal, with its striking black and white markings and formidable presence, has captured the hearts and imaginations of people around the globe.

Throughout the pages of this book, we've ventured into the intricate world of orcas, uncovering their mysteries, marveling at their intelligence, and contemplating the ethical challenges surrounding their existence. We've delved into their origins, their intricate societies, their communication, and their remarkable adaptations. We've explored their roles as bioindicators of ocean health and the urgent need for their conservation.

Yet, as we conclude our journey through the life of these magnificent creatures, we are left with both a sense of wonder and a profound responsibility. Orcas, like so many species on our planet, face challenges born from human activities – pollution, habitat degradation, overfishing, and climate change. Their well-being is inextricably linked to the health of our oceans, and their plight serves as a stark reminder of the fragility of our marine ecosystems.

The epilog of the orca's story is one that calls for action. It calls upon us to recognize the interconnectedness of all life on Earth and the vital role that orcas play in the web of existence. It reminds us that the fate of these magnificent creatures rests in our hands, as stewards of this planet.

In the epilog, we find hope. We see the tireless efforts of scientists, conservationists, and advocates striving to protect and preserve orcas and their habitats. We witness the awakening of public consciousness, a growing recognition that the oceans are not an infinite resource to be exploited but a fragile realm to be cherished and safeguarded.

The future of orcas is intertwined with our own. Their survival relies on our commitment to sustainable practices, our advocacy for policy changes, and our collective will to confront the environmental challenges that threaten their existence. It calls for a harmonious coexistence between humanity and the natural world, where the health of our oceans and the well-being of all species are valued above short-term gains.

As we pen this epilog, let us remember that the story of orcas is not yet complete. Their narrative continues to unfold in the waves and currents of our oceans. The choices we make today, the actions we take, and the alliances we forge will shape the chapters that follow.

May the epilog of the orca's tale be one of hope, resilience, and renewal. May it be a testament to our capacity for compassion, understanding, and change. And may it be a lasting reminder that our actions, no matter how small, have the power to shape the destiny of these iconic creatures and the future of our planet's blue heart.

Thank you for taking the time to read our book on orcas. We hope you found it informative, engaging, and inspiring. Your interest in these magnificent marine mammals and the broader issues of conservation and ocean health is greatly appreciated.

If you enjoyed our book and found it valuable, we kindly ask for your support in the form of a positive review. Your feedback not only encourages us but also helps others discover and benefit from this important information. Please consider sharing your thoughts on what you found most compelling or how this book may have influenced your perspective.

Once again, thank you for your time and consideration. Your support in spreading awareness about orcas and the urgent need for their conservation is truly meaningful.

Printed in Great Britain
by Amazon

33748141R00050